Extreme Animals

FANTASTIC FISH

Isabel Thomas

Raintree

Chicago, Illinois

www.capstonepub.com
Visit our website to find out more information about Heinemann-Raintree books.

To order:

☎ Phone 800-747-4992
💻 Visit www.capstonepub.com
  to browse our catalog and order online.

Edited by Daniel Nunn, John-Paul Wilkins, and Rebecca Rissman
Designed by Philippa Jenkins
Picture research by Elizabeth Alexander
Production by Victoria Fitzgerald

Originated by Capstone Global Library
Printed and bound in China by CTPS

16 15 14 13 12
10 9 8 7 6 5 4 3 2 1

Library of Congress Cataloging-in-Publication Data

Cataloging-in-Publication data is on file at the Library of Congress.

ISBN:

978-1-4109-4680-5 (HC) 978-1-4109-4686-7 (PB)

Acknowledgments

We would like to thank the following for permission to reproduce photographs: Alamy pp. 17 (© Reinhard Dirscherl), 25 (© iSpice); Getty Images p. 21 (Max Gibbs/Oxford Scientific); iStockphoto p. 14 (© Chris Dascher); Nature Picture Library pp. 8 (Kim Taylor), 11 (Mark Bowler), 12 (© Alex Mustard),18 (Jane Burton); NHPA pp. 13 (Franco Banfi), 27 (Daniel Heuclin); Photolibrary pp. 4 (Lawson Wood/Nomad), 6 (Mark Strickland/WaterFrame - Underwater Images), 9 (Hugh Clark/FLPA), 10 (Reinhard H), 15 (Andre Seale/ WaterFrame - Underwater Images), 19 (Rodger Jackman/OSF), 20 (Mark Conlin/OSF), 24 (Sylvain Cordier/Bios); Photoshot pp. 7 (© NHPA), 26 (© Oceans-Image/Mark Bowler); Shutterstock pp. 5 (© Khoroshunova Olga), 16 (© Krzysztof Odziomek), 22 (© ligio), 23 (© Jung Hsuan).

Main cover photograph of boxfish reproduced with permission of Shutterstock (© Khoroshunova Olga). Background cover photograph of blue water reproduced with permission of Shutterstock (© Marino).

Some words are shown in bold, **like this**. You can find out what they mean by looking in the glossary.

Contents

Extreme Fish

Do you think you know everything about fish? Think again! All fish live in water and have **gills** and **fins**. But the differences between fish are what make them **extreme**.

Extreme body parts help this frogfish to hide.

Some fish don't need to hide. The bright colors of this boxfish warn **predators** that it is poisonous.

Strange features or behavior may help fish to find **mates** or food—or to avoid getting eaten themselves!

Fish That Go Fishing

Anglerfish have fishing poles growing from their heads. There are even fake worms at the end! **Prey** swim over to eat the "worms." They find out it is a trap when the fish's jaws go "snap"!

fake worm

DID YOU KNOW?

Deep sea anglerfish have two sets of teeth. The second set is in their throat. These teeth stop prey from escaping.

Armed Archerfish

Archerfish do not wait for **prey** to come to them. They use their mouths like a squirt gun and shoot it down!

Archerfish can shoot jets of water 10 times longer than their bodies. That is like spitting a mouthful of water from one side of a swimming pool to the other!

If prey is close enough, archerfish leap out of the water to grab it.

Adventurous Eels

Eels are fish that like to break rules.
Some eels can:

- swim backward
- change from males into females
- leave the water and wriggle over land
- sneak into gardens to eat vegetables and earthworms.

Freshwater eels are born in the Atlantic and Pacific oceans. The baby eels swim across the ocean to find rivers to live in. Their journey takes up to two years.

What a Shock!

Electric eels have a special skill. They can give **prey** an electric shock! This **paralyzes** the prey and makes it easy to eat.

An electric eel's tail is four times the length of its head and body. It uses its tail to make electricity.

head and body

tail

The shock from an electric eel is big enough to knock a horse off its feet!

Shark Bites

A shark's teeth are replaced often. This keeps them very sharp. A tiger shark can bite through the shell of a sea turtle! It eats everything it can find.

DID YOU KNOW?

All of these things have been found in the stomachs of tiger sharks:

- suit of armor
- half a crocodile
- hen house full of chickens
- rubber tire
- a missing sailor.

How do you hide from a hammerhead shark? Standing in the dark while being completely still and silent will not help. The shark will be able to sense your heartbeat!

The hammerhead shark's weird head is very sensitive. It can sense tiny amounts of electricity in the bodies of fish. Even a fish buried under sand cannot hide!

ray buried in sand

Don't Step on a Stonefish!

Stonefish are one of the most deadly fish in the world. Their **venomous spines** can kill a human. When **prey** swims past, stonefish attack so fast that a normal video camera cannot record it.

venomous spines

eye

The stonefish's amazing camouflage makes it look like rock or coral.

Fishy Whiskers

A catfish is like a giant, swimming tongue. Its body is covered in taste buds. It has the best sense of taste in the animal world. It uses **barbels** around its mouth to find food. A catfish can taste a meal before it catches it!

barbel

DID YOU KNOW?

Vampire catfish are tiny but mean. They swim into the **gills** of larger fish and feast on their blood.

Prickly Porcupine Fish

Small fish need to avoid being eaten. Porcupine fish can make themselves impossible to swallow. They puff up their bodies by sucking in water or air. In seconds, they are two or three times bigger. Their long **spines** can stick out up to 2 inches.

Fantastic Flying Fish

Flying fish have an **extreme** way to escape **predators**. They disappear! They do this by leaping out of the water. Their enormous **fins** allow them to glide through the air.

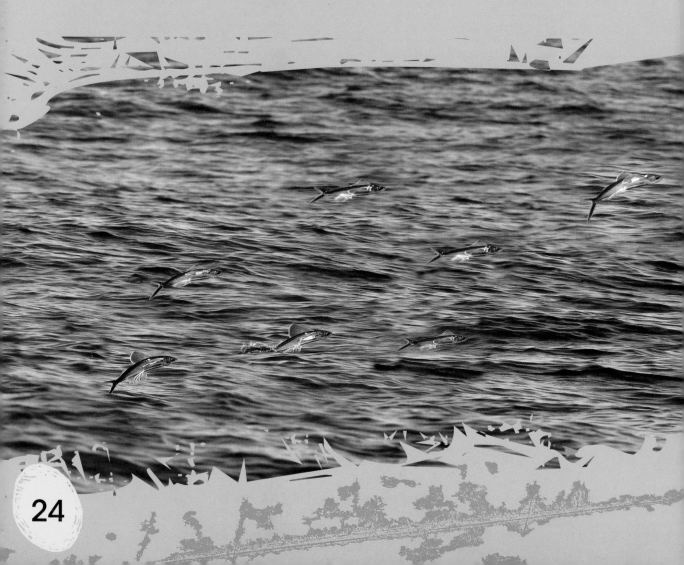

fin

Flying fish beat their tails against the water as they glide. They can stay in the air for 45 seconds.

Unstoppable Lungfish

Lack of rain is bad news for most fish. Their **gills** only work underwater. But lungfish can breathe air, too. When their river or lake dries up, lungfish bury themselves in a **mucus cocoon**. Lungfish can survive inside the dried mucus for more than four years.

lungfish

mucus cocoon

Record-Breakers

Which fish do you think is the most **extreme**? Why? Take a look at some of these record-breaking fish to help you decide.

What? Flying fish

Why? Longest journey out of water

Wow! Flying fish can leap up to 33 feet above the water. That is about the height of five doors on top of each other!

What? Piranha

Why? Most people eaten by fish in one sitting

Wow! In 1981 a boat sank in Brazil. Piranhas killed and ate more than 300 passengers.

What? Whale shark

Why? Largest fish

Wow! These monsters of the deep can grow to be about 40 feet long. That is as long as a big school bus!

What? Frilled shark

Why? World's longest pregnancy

Wow! Each frilled shark pregnancy lasts for up to three-and-a-half years!

What? Death puffer

Why? Most poisonous to eat

Wow! The poisonous skin, blood, and liver of puffer fish can kill a person in just 20 minutes. They are popular meals in Japan—with the poisonous parts removed!

What? Orange roughy

Why? Longest-living

Wow! These slow-growing fish often live to celebrate their 150th birthdays!

Glossary

barbel whisker-like body part on the heads of certain fish, such as catfish

camouflage colors or markings that help an animal to blend in with the things around it

cocoon case or covering used to protect an animal

extreme unusual, amazing, or different from normal

fin thin, flat body part of a fish, used for swimming

gill body part for breathing, used by fish and other animals that live in water

mate animal that can have babies together with another animal

mucus thick, slimy liquid used to protect certain parts of an animal's body

paralyze take away the ability to move

predator animal that hunts other animals for food

prey animal that is hunted by another animal for food

spine sharp, pointed body part that sticks out on some animals

venomous able to produce venom, or poison

Find Out More

Books

Meinking, Mary. *Shark vs. Penguin* (Predator vs. Prey). Chicago: Raintree, 2011.

Schreiber, Anne. *Sharks!* (Science Readers). Washington, D.C.: National Geographic, 2008.

Solway, Andrew. *Killer Fish* (Wild Predators). Chicago: Heinemann Library, 2005.

Web sites

Check out some amazing facts and photographs of the puffer fish at this web site:
kids.nationalgeographic.com/kids/animals/creaturefeature/pufferfish

Find answers to lots of questions about sharks at this web site:
www.sdnhm.org/kids/sharks/faq.html

Index